STAGECOACH WEST SCOTLAND

DAVID DEVOY

AMBERLEY

First published 2019

Amberley Publishing
The Hill, Stroud
Gloucestershire, GL5 4EP

www.amberley-books.com

Copyright © David Devoy, 2019

The right of David Devoy to be identified as
the Author of this work has been asserted in
accordance with the Copyrights, Designs and
Patents Act 1988.

ISBN 978 1 4456 9167 1 (print)
ISBN 978 1 4456 9168 8 (ebook)

British Library Cataloguing in Publication Data.
A catalogue record for this book is available from
the British Library.

Origination by Amberley Publishing.
Printed in the UK.

Introduction

Stagecoach West Scotland is an operating region of Stagecoach UK Bus, running as Western Buses Ltd, and based in Ayr. It operates in west, central and south-west Scotland, in an area bounded by Greenock and Braehead to the north, Hamilton to the east, Carlisle to the south and the Isle of Arran to the west. Frequent express services also reach Glasgow from throughout Ayrshire.

Stagecoach West Scotland has operated under various brands; Stagecoach Western is the prevalent brand and is used for the vast majority of bus operations throughout the region. Stagecoach A1 Service was a trading name of Western Buses Ltd, and was used for the trunk service between Ardrossan and Kilmarnock that came with the purchase of the independent A1 Service business. Vehicles running under this brand wore a blue and cream livery until June 2010. Stagecoach in Glasgow branding was used for services within Glasgow and those from Glasgow to Cumbernauld. The Magicbus brand was also used for services in the city at various times. In addition, vehicles operating on the former AA Buses services, in the Irvine area, previously wore the historical AA green and cream livery, though there never was a Stagecoach AA Buses brand. The company also provides vehicles for Scottish Citylink express work, mainly on the Glasgow to Edinburgh corridor.

Stagecoach operated in Glasgow as Magicbus in 1986 after deregulation, using old London AEC Routemaster buses, though it sold the operation to Kelvin Central Buses in the early 1990s.

In June 1994 Stagecoach Holdings made a £6 million offer to purchase loss-making Western Scottish Buses from its staff and management. Agreement was reached in August, and events moved swiftly. Western's registered office was changed from London to Frenchwood Avenue, Preston; this was the same address as Ribble. The first ten new buses were obtained with deliveries reallocated from other group subsidiaries, and the corporate white livery with red/orange and blue stripes was adopted for the fleet.

Arran Transport and Trading was purchased on 1 October, which added twenty-four vehicles to the fleet, operating from a depot in Brodick. New premises were also obtained in Dunoon. Agreement with Clyde Coast limited competition around Kilmarnock, and Shuttle Buses withdrew from service operations from the middle of the month. Meanwhile, Stagecoach launched services in Glasgow in competition with Strathclyde Buses in November. A batch of new vehicles had been stored in Aberdeen prior to the launch. The company came to a deal with Strathclyde Buses very quickly and a 20 per cent stake was taken, with eighteen of the new buses passing to SBL as part of the deal.

On 29 January 1995 the Ayrshire Bus Owners (A1 Service) Ltd joined the Stagecoach Empire for a sum of £4.25 million, adding around eighty vehicles, an office and a bus stand located at Parkhouse Road, Ardrossan. Four new directors were appointed and comprised two each from Stagecoach Holdings and Western Scottish Buses. Existing premises in Harbour Road, Ardrossan, were reactivated to house the acquired fleet. The company was renamed as Stagecoach (A1 Service) Ltd from 9 February.

Meanwhile, Western faced an inquiry from the Office of Fair Trading regarding competition with Carrick Coaches between Ayr and Patna/Dalmellington. The decision meant that Western was banned from operating on the corridor for a period of one year from 28 February. However, the independent AA Buses registered the journeys in place of Western. A batch of former London Leyland Titans were drafted into the A1 fleet to replace many non-standard and time-expired vehicles, while a batch of twenty-one brand-new Volvo Olympians were due for delivery around May/June 1995. Further vehicles were brought in from other group subsidiaries to replace more former A1 buses. A legal move saw the Arran Transport and Company Ltd renamed as Clyde Islands Bus Company Ltd, but it did not own any vehicles and was in the process of being wound up. Service numbers were allocated to the former A1 routes with numbers 11 and 21 being used on the Ardrossan/Kilmarnock and Kilmarnock/Irvine services respectively. Other numbers included 12/18/20/21/24 and 27. New buses continued to join the Western fleet with Volvo B6s and B10Ms arriving. The Stagecoach Express name made its debut on the X77 service. A1 received its first brand-new buses in June when four new Volvo B10Ms arrived. Two carried corporate colours while the other pair carried a livery of white with two green bands, and Coastlink 535 lettering. The service was in competition with Ashton Coaches and linked Greenock to Ayr. It was run by a consortium consisting of AA Buses/A1 Service and Clydeside 2000. A1 dropped out from August, but their journeys were replaced by Clyde Coast Services, who borrowed the buses A1 had used on the route. The business of Hamilton of Maybole was acquired by Western, although a couple of buses passed to A1 Service and operated out of the Ayr depot of Western. Clyde Coast withdrew their Saltcoats to Irvine service on 4 August and purchased a batch of former A1 Volvo Ailsas from Stagecoach to operate school services that had been won on tender. A1 Service took over all the Clyde Coast local services from the beginning of September along with four minibuses.

The company also replaced The Valley Bus Co. on the Dalry to Irvine and Dalry local services after that company had their licence revoked. Ashton Coaches claimed that the 535 consortium was using 'copycat' tactics to confuse passengers by using similar colours and route numbers. The court upheld the claim and the consortium were ordered to change the colour of the buses used on the route. Initially the buses were run in white, but new branding using red and the fleet name ClydeCoaster was adopted. Clyde Coast provided five buses for the service; AA Buses, two; and Clydeside 2000 a further pair. Another competitor in the Irvine area had its licence revoked and Wynter-M ceased operations. It was announced that The Monopoly and Mergers Commission would investigate the A1 takeover as competition concerns had arisen. The company agreed to various undertakings, and released the former A1 directors from their covenants barring them from competing for a period of three years. A new open-top tour of the Isle of Arran was registered from 9 June by Western. Planning permission was applied for in regard to the redevelopment of Kilmarnock depot. Part of the site was to be sold off and a new entrance built on Mackinlay Place. A new service number, X16, linking Ardrossan and Edinburgh, commenced in mid-October.

January 1996 saw the A1 operation move to a larger depot at the former P&O Pandora premises at Ardrossan Harbour. AA Buses withdrew from the Ayr to Dalmellington route in favour of Western once again, as their one-year ban was up. The former A1 commuter routes linking Ayrshire to Glasgow were transferred to Western and allocated numbers X33/4/5. New buses continued to join the fleet on a regular basis throughout the year. The buses used on the

Butlins Holiday Camp to Ayr town centre service were outshopped in a special advertising livery. Service frequencies were improved on the Drongan/Ayr corridor to compete more vigorously with similar facilities provided by Keenan of Ayr. The Dumfries to Glasgow service, X2, had the frequency doubled at the end of May, and the company announced that the head office would move from Kilmarnock to Ayr in August. In Glasgow Strathclyde Buses was sold to FirstGroup, and Stagecoach sold their 20 per cent stake to the new owners at a substantial profit of around £15 million. Stagecoach (A1 Service) Ltd was renamed as A1 Service Ltd at the end of June, with the registered address being Sandgate, Ayr. The former A1 bus stance at Parkhouse Road in Ardrossan was sold for redevelopment in August. As part of the same process Western Buses Ltd was formed and used the same address in Ayr. A new open-top tour was launched on the Isle of Bute, and a heritage bus service was added to the Arran network. New-style red fleet names were used by both Western and A1. The last bus in the old A1 blue and cream was due for a repaint in October and took everyone by surprise when it emerged redone in the traditional A1 livery. Even more remarkable was the repainting of one of the corporate-liveried Volvo Olympians into blue and cream. It was then decided that the main A1 Service would be run by buses in this livery, which was similar to the old A1 livery. The reason was not apparent at the time, but events later would show this to be an astute move.

In February 1997 Stagecoach registered a new subsidiary at the Sandgate headquarters in Ayr. The company was named Schoolbus Ltd with an allowance of forty vehicles. This was a subterfuge, as in March Stagecoach announced that it was going to have another attempt to share in the Glasgow bus market. £10 million was to be invested in developing new services, and this would create around 250 jobs. The first routes began in April and were followed by more in May. A depot was obtained at Dunblane Street in the city to house a fleet of brand-new buses. Initially services X8/9/10 were operated under the Western licence but later transferred to Stagecoach Glasgow. Firstbus was not slow to retaliate and registered some new routes where it thought Stagecoach might strike next. But the biggest shock was the registration by their Kelvin subsidiary to operate on the former main Ardrossan to Kilmarnock route; the reason for Stagecoach using the traditional colours now became apparent. Firstbus managed to obtain a batch of new low-floor buses to operate this at short notice, giving them a slight advantage. A total of 18 Dennis Darts were operated from the premises of local independent Eagle Coaches in Stevenston. Firstbus also ramped up frequencies on the Glasgow to Cumbernauld corridor in competition with Stagecoach subsidiary Fife Scottish. Stagecoach was quick to purchase the business of AA Buses at the end of June, preventing Firstbus from gaining another foothold in the area. Forty-one buses were added to the fleet. Firstbus, however, retaliated by registering FirstFife service 56, linking Edinburgh to Dunfermline and Ballingry. This was operated by their Lowland subsidiary, and used Westfield depot in Edinburgh and a small yard in Halbeath. From 7 July all A1 buses had the legal lettering changed to Western Buses Ltd. Elsewhere, Clydeside 2000 acquired the business of Ashton Coaches on 14 July. Western added short-workings of service 4 in Glasgow between Newton Mearns and the city centre. The local service of Paterson's of Dalry was taken over by Western, as were the local routes operated by Shuttle Buses in Kilmarnock and Irvine areas. The AA livery was retained for some buses and modern acquisitions were given the green and cream colours with a cream AA Buses fleet name in the same font as the other fleet names used by the group.

April 1998 saw Western take over the limited stop services of Crawford of Neilston between Ayrshire and Glasgow. These routes began in 1980 when Bennetts of Kilwinning and A1 Service registered the services. Bennetts later sold their service to Stagecoach of Perth, who later decided that, although profitable, it was out on a limb and decided to sell the operation to Crawford's of Neilston! In Glasgow some retrenchment took place when Stagecoach withdrew from

Cardonald, Milton and Clydebank. An open-top tour of Dumfries was operated in the summer season. Western provided buses for the Tall Ships Race between Greenock Victoria Harbour and Ardgowan from 30 July to 2 August. Western launched a pair of midi-Dennis Darts on 19 August at a ceremony in Whithorn to mark the signing of a quality partnership between the company and Dumfries and Galloway Council. The ClydeCoaster livery and branding was discontinued from September. It was announced in October 1999 that the A1 name would be confined to the vehicles wearing the blue and cream livery, with all other buses adopting the Western fleet name in corporate style. Stagecoach Glasgow purchased the business of Owen's of Chapelhall in October. This business traded as Scottish Highway Express and provided a link between Glasgow and Edinburgh in competition with Scottish Citylink Coaches. It was run under the Schoolbus Scotland licence briefly before being transferred to Stagecoach Glasgow.

2000 saw Western hit by a series of one-day strikes by drivers during March, after rejecting a proposed settlement. Strathclyde Passenger Transport drafted in over eighty buses to maintain school contracts and services in Ayrshire and Arran. As a cost-cutting measure Stagecoach Glasgow withdrew services X8/9/10 from Buchanan bus station to save departure fees, and used a terminal point in Renfield Street instead. Meanwhile services 20 and X74 were linked to provide a through service linking Drumchapel to Castlemilk, thus avoiding Buchanan bus station for the same reasons. Western closed Girvan depot from 19 August in a cost-cutting measure. It was announced that services based on Annan would be transferred to Stagecoach Cumberland, while service X73, Annan to Edinburgh, was to be renumbered as X100. It was decided to refresh the corporate identity with a new colour scheme designed by Ray Stenning, essentially using the same colours, but in a drastically different layout, which came to be known as 'beachball' livery. Minor competition existed for several years from T. & E. Docherty around Irvine, and from Shuttle Buses between Irvine and Girdle Toll, along with local operations around Kilmarnock and Irvine.

The first bus repainted into the new corporate scheme was Dennis Dart number 460, which had been in AA Buses livery. This seems a good point to leave our story here for now, and hopefully it will be continued.

Thanks as always go to my daughters Sammi and Jenny for their help in this project, and of course to all my friends in the industry.

EGT 458T was a Leyland National 11351A/3R B33T, new to British Airways, at Heathrow Airport in July 1978, although it had been delivered as WGY598S. This had been changed before its entry into service. On disposal, in 1993, it passed to Western Buses and was rebuilt to B48F and re-registered as UIB 3076. This view shows it working in Rothesay on the Isle of Bute, located in the Clyde Estuary. It carries Stagecoach fleet names but still retains its old livery.

When Stagecoach acquired Western, they quickly announced that new buses would join the fleet. The initial batch was diverted from a Fife order and entered service in stripes, but without any fleet names. M676 SSX was a Volvo B6-50/Alexander Dash B40F, delivered new as Western V353 in August 1994, and snapped at Ayr bus station. It would later run on Merseyside with Glenvale Transport.

ECS 882V was a Leyland Fleetline FE30AGR/Northern Counties H44/31F, new as Western Scottish R2882 in October, 1979. It is shown in Stagecoach days at Stranraer depot. It would be acquired by Rapson's Coaches in 1999. The Northern Counties Motor & Engineering Company was founded in Wigan in 1919 by Henry Lewis. In 1967, fellow bodybuilder Massey Brothers, located in nearby Pemberton, was acquired and became a part of the Northern Counties operations. The Massey factory was retained and used as a paint shop and for final completion of bodywork assembled at Wigan Lane.

After the acquisition of A1 Service in 1995, a batch of Alexander R Type-bodied Volvo Olympians was diverted from Cumberland to replace many non-standard vehicles. They were delivered in corporate livery, as shown by N862 VHH, but it was always the intention that they would wear a version of blue and cream and they were repainted as soon as was practical.

C647 LFT was a Leyland Olympian ONLXB/1R/Alexander R Type H77F, new to Tyne and Wear PTE as their number 647 in March 1986. It passed to Stagecoach with the acquisition of Busways and was transferred to Glasgow. It is loading in Osborne Street for the service to Castlemilk. It later served with Western in Ayrshire before disposal to McColl's Coaches, where it received fleet number 3036.

After Graham's of Paisley ceased to trade – the fleet was auctioned in June 1990 – HGD 213T did not stray too far, for it was purchased by Robert Steele for his A1 Service fleet. It passed with the services to Stagecoach in 1995, and is seen in Irvine with Stagecoach fleet names. It later worked for Cheyne's of Daviot and Watermill Coaches of Fraserburgh.

K574 DFS was a Volvo B10M-60/Plaxton Interurban C53F, purchased new by Stagecoach Fife as fleet number 574 in March 1993. I remember being most impressed with them at the time; however it was transferred to Western in 1995, and is seen leaving Glasgow bound for Cumnock. It would later pass to Abus of Liverpool as 803HOM.

YSF 98S was a Leyland Leopard PSU3D/4R/Alexander Y Type B53F, new as Alexander (Fife) fleet number FPE98 in October 1977. It became Fife Scottish number 98 and passed with the business to Stagecoach. It was one of a pair transferred to the former A1 operations in 1995, and was captured in Kilmarnock.

N616 VSS was a Mercedes 709D/Alexander B25F, new as Western 016 in January 1996, shown with A1 Service fleet names. It would later become Cambus number 206. It would then join the Cumberland fleet as their number 40616. The second generation of the Mercedes T2 range was introduced in 1986, and was significantly upgraded, the bonnet having become longer and altogether more sharp-edged. The chassis sold in large numbers in the United Kingdom during the minibus revolution. Variations included the 609D, 614D, 709D, 711D, 811D, and 814D.

A308 RSU was a Volvo Citybus B10M-50/East Lancs H83F, new as a Volvo Demonstrator in January 1983. It joined the fleet of A1 Service member Docherty of Irvine and passed with the business to Stagecoach A1 Service. On disposal it saw further service with Marshalls of Baillieston and DJ International of Barrhead.

M871 ASW was a Volvo B10M-55/Alexander PS Type DP48F, delivered new as Stagecoach A1 Service number 507 in June 1995. It was caught loading in Irvine while working on service 11, bound for Ardrossan, although the screen is set at number 12. It would later pass to the main fleet and receive fleet number 20507 in the national series. It would later join Keenan of Ayr as a school bus.

L144 VRH was a Dennis Dart/Plaxton Pointer B34F, purchased new by London Buses Ltd as their DRL144 in November 1993. It passed to the privatised Stagecoach East London fleet in September 1994 and joined Western in January 2000. This view shows it loading in Ayr. On disposal in July 2002, it passed to Canavan of Croy.

B198 CGA was a Volvo B10M-61/Berhof Esprite C53F, purchased new by Western Scottish as their V198 in February 1985. It was purchased at a time when Western were doing business with Ensign (dealer) and was convertible to C49Ft. Time-expired buses were traded in and this fine coach was supplied in exchange. It was caught turning into Bath Street in Glasgow whilst bound for Sanquhar.

E866 RCS was a Volvo Citybus B10M-50/Alexander R Type CH80F, purchased new by Western Scottish as their V266 in December 1987. It later worked for Magicbus in Glasgow, then Megabus before being demoted as a school bus. It was captured in Ayr. The Citybus double-decker version of the B10M was launched in early 1982, with a down-rated engine from the coach chassis.

ASA 9Y was a Leyland Tiger TRCTL112R/Duple Dominant II Express C49F, new to Northern Scottish as their fleet number NCT9 in February 1983. It was re-registered as TSV779, but this was changed to CSO 390Y on its disposal to Stagecoach Western in 1995. It is seen at Stranraer depot carrying Stagecoach Express decals.

M726 BCS was a Volvo B6-50/Alexander Dash DP40F, purchased new by Stagecoach Western in August 1994. It was photographed in Ayr whilst working on the 585 Coastliner service. The Volvo B6 was a 5.5-litre-engined midibus chassis manufactured by Volvo between 1991 and 1999. The initial pre-production series of around thirty chassis were manufactured by Volvo subsidiary Steyr Bus GmbH in Vienna, Austria. This would, however, not be the case with the production series, as Volvo moved it to Scotland.

D218 NCS was a Dennis Dorchester SDA811/Alexander TC Type C55F, new to Western Scottish as N218 in April 1987. It survived into the Stagecoach era and is seen resplendent in its stripes whilst working on tour duties on the Isle of Bute on a beautiful summer's day. In the background is an ex-Arran Transport Bedford. It would later see further service with Rowe and Tudhope, JJ Travel of Coatbridge, Bennetts of Kilwinning and Tees Valley, ending up as a seventy-seater.

WYV 27T was a Leyland Titan TNLXB2RRsp/Park Royal H66D, new as London Regional Transport T27 in May 1979. It was photographed on a short-lived service which added short-workings to service 4 and increased competition with First Glasgow and City Sprinter. However, it had one great weakness: the buses were taken off at around three o'clock to go and do school contracts, which meant that when the service should have been busy, it didn't run, which really seemed pointless, and no doubt led to its early demise.

P374 DSA was a Volvo B6LE-53/Alexander ALX200 DP36F, purchased new by Western Buses as their fleet number 374 in April 1997. It was intended for service in Glasgow but was used in Kilmarnock before the Glasgow invasion began. It would later return to Ayrshire and was given AA Buses livery for a while. On disposal it passed to McColl's Coaches as their 2047.

XUF534Y was a Leyland Tiger TRCTL11/3R/Plaxton Paramount 3200 C50F, new to Southdown in May 1983 as their 1004. It was re-registered as 404DCD using a plate from an old Leyland Titan. On disposal it became BYJ 919Y and did a brief stint with Western. It is seen at Dumfries, Whitesands, ready to do a run to Kirkcudbright on service 76.

L208 PSB was a Dennis Dart/Marshall C36 B39F new to Arran Transport and Trading, which was based in Brodick on the Isle of Arran in June 1994, and passed to Stagecoach with the business. It was photographed at Dunoon depot. The whole front end had to be rebuilt later on following an accident, and repaired using Plaxton parts.

M481 ASW was a Volvo B10M-55/Alexander PS Type DP48F, new to Stagecoach A1 Service in June 1995. It is seen here working in the Arran fleet, leaving Brodick for the north of the island, with the CALMAC Ferry *Caledonian Isles* in the background. This combination was the Stagecoach standard for many years and was very reliable, and fuel-efficient in service.

B24 CGA was a Volvo Citybus B10M-50/Alexander RV Type H47/37F, purchased new by A1
Service member Robert Meney in March 1985. It served just short of ten years before passing to
Stagecoach with the business, and duly received its stripes. It carried A1 fleet names for most of
its time, but did receive the red Western block names briefly. This view was taken in Ardrossan.
The bus would later serve with McColl's and DJ International.

GCS 38V was a Leyland Leopard PSU3E/4R/Alexander Y type B53F, purchased new by Western
Scottish as their AL38 in March 1980. It lasted long enough to receive its stripes and was looking
good as it headed out of Ayr for Dalmellington on route 51. On disposal it would remain in
Ayrshire with Keenan's of Coalhall under the alias of WDS 343V.

R36 LSO was a Mercedes-Benz Vario 0814/Plaxton Beaver B27F, new to Stagecoach Glasgow in July 1997. It was photographed whilst working on service 7 at the Pollok Centre in Glasgow. It was thought at the time that this might have been the first of many, but this proved to be wrong. It later saw service with Stagecoach Western in Ayrshire, with Cumberland as number 36, and with Ribble as number 42000.

N850 VHH was a Volvo YN2R/Alexander R Type H47/32F, new as Stagecoach A1 Service number 916 in August 1995. Although delivered in corporate stripes, it had received blue and cream by the time of this shot, taken in Ardrossan. It was looking a bit rough as many stone chips allowed the original white to show through.

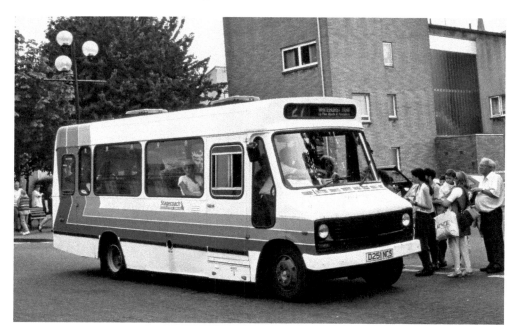

D251 NCS was a Dodge S56/Alexander B25F, delivered new as Western Scottish D251 in April 1987. The type was popular with the Scottish Bus Group as it was readily available and had an automatic gearbox, which allowed new drivers to be recruited quickly. It is seen later in life with Stagecoach A1 Service fleet names while loading in Irvine.

EYE 246V was a Leyland Titan TNLXB2RRSP/Park Royal H44/24D, delivered new as London Transport T246 in May 1980. It was originally ordered by Maidstone & District as their intended number 5266, registered as BKJ 266T, then was later intended to be 5396, registered as FKM 396V. It passed to Stagecoach Western and is seen in Ayr wearing Butlins Wonderwest colours.

When Stagecoach decided to reintroduce the blue and cream colours to service 11, this was the first attempt. It was not deemed as a success and was repainted with more cream on the upper deck. It was thought that this livery was introduced to deter former A1 members from restarting stage services, but hindsight shows it was done in case Firstbus decided to retaliate after services were launched in Glasgow.

F524 WSJ was an all-Leyland Olympian ONCL10/1RZ H47/31F, purchased new by A1 Service member Hill of Ardrossan in January 1989. It passed to Stagecoach with the business, and is shown in Irvine carrying an unusual front-end livery treatment, which was later changed for the standard version.

B83 WUV was an all-Leyland Titan TNLXB2RR H44/26D, new as London Transport T1083 in September 1994. It passed to Stagecoach Selkent in September 1994 and was converted to open-top, single-door OH44/29F layout in December 1997. It was transferred to Western Scottish as their number 972 in April 1998, and is shown lettered for the Arran tour.

H789 GTA was a Mercedes-Benz 811D/Carlyle C19 B29F, new to Red Admiral as their number 789 in July 1991. When Carlyle closed down, the bodywork designs were sold to Marshall's of Cambridge. This bus came into Stagecoach ownership with the purchase of Transit Holdings, and is seen running in Clydebank during the Glasgow bus wars.

R461 LSO was a Dennis Dart SLF/ALX 200 B37F, new as Stagecoach Western number 461 in February 1998. It is seen loading in Irvine while working on the former AA Buses service to Ayr. It was later transferred to East Midland for further service.

When Stagecoach bought out the operations of A1 Service in 1995 not all vehicles were included, but HGD 213T was. It was photographed at Ardrossan depot, and would survive with Stagecoach for a little over two years before being sold to Cheyne's of Daviot in July 1997, and later to Watermill of Fraserburgh in 2002. This bus was a Leyland Atlantean AN68A/1R/ Alexander H78F, new to Graham's of Paisley in April 1979, and built on a production line of similar buses for Glasgow as an extra.

L208 PSB was a Dennis Dart/Marshall C36 B39F, new to Arran Transport, based in Brodick, in June 1994, and passed to Stagecoach with the business. Unfortunately it was involved in an argument with a wall in August 1999. It was repaired with a Plaxton Pointer front end, which blended quite well with the rest of the bodywork. This view shows it in service after transfer to Rothesay depot but still lacking fleet names.

UNA 824S was a Leyland Atlantean AN68A/1R/Park Royal H43/32F, new as Greater Manchester PTE number 7824 in August 1977. It passed to Western Scottish after the demise of Dickson's of Dumfries, but is shown after transfer to the Stagecoach A1 fleet. It was ready for service at Ardrossan depot. 'Gouranga' is a Hare Krishna mantra meaning 'be happy'.

R469 LSO was a Dennis Dart SLF/Alexander ALX200 B37F, new as Stagecoach Western number 469 in November 1997. It is seen working in Irvine after being repainted into AA Buses livery, maintaining the illusion that it was still a local independent company. It later became Stagecoach Hull number 33769.

B196 CGA was a Volvo B10M-61/Plaxton Paramount 3500 C46Ft purchased new by Western Scottish as their V196 in May 1985. It served with Clydeside Scottish before returning to Western in 1989. It was C51F when captured in Dumfries at Buccleuch Street Bridge, wearing Stagecoach Express livery.

R821 YUD was a Dennis Dart SLF/Alexander ALX200 B37F, purchased new by Thames Transit as their number 821 in February 1998. It was transferred to Western in 1999 and is seen in Ayr working on local Ayr service A1. It later became 33821 in the national fleet numbering series and saw further service with Stagecoach Oxford and Stagecoach Midland Red.

Let me share my personal favourite Stagecoach picture of all time. It shows M151 FGB working on The ClydeCoaster as she cruises through the Ayrshire coastal resort of Largs. She was a Volvo B10B-58/Wright Endurance B51F, new to A1 Service member Docherty of Irvine in November 1994 as M1 ABO. This was a cherished number plate, which stood for 'Ayrshire Bus Owners'. The original plate was retained by the Docherty family when the services were taken over by Stagecoach in 1995.

M483 ASW was a Volvo B10M-55/Alexander PS Type DP48F, purchased new
by Stagecoach A1 Service in June 1995. It was passing through Greenock on the
Coastlink 535 Service. The branding had to be removed after a court action by Ashton
Coaches of Greenock, who felt it was too close to their branding. For a short while
the buses ran in all-over white before the red stripes and ClydeCoaster branding was
applied. The bus was later renumbered as number 20511 and would see service with
Stagecoach in Glasgow and in the Highlands.

BCS 865T was a Leyland Fleetline FE30AGR/Northern Counties H75F, purchased
new by Western Scottish as their R2865 in May 1979. It survived long enough to
receive Stagecoach stripes and looked stunning with the fitting of wheel trims, which
really set it off. It was allocated to Dumfries depot.

S49 RGA was a MAN 11.220/Marshall B36F, new to Dart Buses in January 1999. It is seen at the Pollok Centre in Glasgow working an X8 for Stagecoach Glasgow under a franchise agreement. At the time Stagecoach owned 20 per cent of Dart, but when it became clear that the company could not carry on financially it was alleged that an appeal for Stagecoach to buy the remaining shares fell on deaf ears, so the directors went to First Glasgow and told them that the buses would come off on whatever day. First made a fleet available at short notice and had the routes quickly registered, much to the annoyance of Stagecoach who seemed to be caught napping for once.

M950 EGE was a Dennis Dart/Plaxton Pointer B40F, purchased new by Dodd's of Ayr in December 1994, and passed to Stagecoach Western in June 1997 as fleet number 401. It was given Stagecoach-style AA lettering, and was passing through Irvine. It would later receive swoops livery as fleet number 32381.

T36 VCS was a Dennis Dart SLF/Plaxton Pointer B29F, purchased new by Western as fleet number 389 in August 1999. It had just arrived in Newton Stewart on a foul day and was preparing to leave for Port William on service 415. It would become 33089 in the national numbering series, and see out its days with Western.

V604 GCS was a MAN 18.220/Alexander ALX200 B42F, purchased new by Stagecoach Western in December 1999. It was later converted to run on biofuel. Stagecoach Perth ran it as their number 22604 after it was converted back to diesel. By 2020, the EU aims to have 10 per cent of the transport fuel of every EU country come from renewable sources such as biofuels. Fuel suppliers are also required to reduce the greenhouse gas intensity of the EU fuel mix by 6 per cent by 2020 in comparison to 2010.

WLT 831 was an AEC Routemaster/Park Royal H36/28R, new as London Transport RM831 in July 1961. It was one of a batch purchased by the fledgling independent Stagecoach of Perth in May 1987. We all wondered as to their eventual deployment and later found out they were to be based in Glasgow under the new Magicbus identity. WLT 831 would later gain fleet number 603 and be re-registered as EDS 341A in August 1988.

C594 SHC was a Mercedes L608D/PMT B20F, new as Southdown number 914 in June 1986. It is seen in an anonymous white livery in Ayr after Stagecoach A1 Service registered services against Carrick Coaches. It would later have corporate stripes applied to the paintwork.

G529 LWU was a Volvo B10M-60/Plaxton Paramount III C50F, purchased new by Wallace Arnold Tours of Leeds in March 1990. On disposal in 1993 it passed to Stagecoach Midland Red (south) as their number 61 and was reseated to C48Ft. It was transferred within the group to Stagecoach Western in 1997 and the seating was changed once again when it became C51F. It was re-registered as VCS 376 in October 1997 and allocated to Dumfries, where this shot was taken. The presentation was superb, especially with wheel trims fitted.

R513 KSA was a Volvo B10M-55/Alexander PS Type B49F, purchased new by Stagecoach Glasgow as their number 513 in August 1997. It was being used in Ayrshire to bolster the A1 fleet in this view taken in Irvine. It would later become number 20513 in the main Western fleet before departing for Stagecoach Cambridge.

MSC 556X was a Leyland Tiger TRCTL11/3R/Duple Goldliner C46Ft, purchased new by Eastern Scottish as their XH 556 in July 1982. It was transferred to Bluebird Buses in 1987 as NCT6 and re-registered as CSU 923. It passed to Stagecoach with the business, becoming number 436 with the registration RRS 225X. After the takeover of A1 Service it was drafted into Ardrossan depot, and was leaving Glasgow on service 34, bound for Largs.

Stagecoach Western ESU 435 was a Volvo B10M, which had been re-bodied in 1994 by East Lancashire Coachbuilders, with an EL2000 body seating fifty-one. It had been new to Western Scottish in April 1982 as GGE 127X, with Duple Goldliner bodywork. It was re-registered FSU 737 and TOS 550X before becoming ESU 435. It was photographed wearing ClydeCoaster livery in Ayr.

G270 TSL was a Mercedes 709D/Alexander B25F, purchased new by Magicbus Glasgow as their number 270 in January 1990. It passed to Stagecoach Bluebird before arriving at Western in 1998, and was allocated to Ardrossan depot. It was passing through the town on service 30 bound for Largs, which would have been run by Clyde Coast in the old days.

These two Leyland Leopard/Alexander Y Type B53Fs were based at Stranraer depot and still looked very smart despite their years. It was always interesting to spot the differences in the paint job, as you just assume that they are all the same.

B577 LPE was a Leyland Olympian ONTL11/2RSp/ECW CH45/28F, new to Alder Valley in January 1985. It passed to Clyde Coast in July 1991 and lasted just over a year. On withdrawal in August 1982 it passed to Cleveland Coaches and was re-registered as PJI 4983. It must have liked Scotland however as it returned in July 1995, this time running for Stagecoach Western until 1998. It was sold to Stephenson's of Rochford in 1999 and then to Tim's Travel of Sheerness in 2000. It was caught in Kilmarnock.

C84 PRP was a Leyland Tiger TRCTL11/3RH/Plaxton Paramount 3500 C46Ft, purchased new by United Counties as their number 84 in April 1986 for National Express work. It was reseated to C51F by Stagecoach South before transfer to Western, and would later become Stagecoach Bluebird number 462.

E645 KYW was an MCW Metrorider MF158/1 B33F, new to London Buses Ltd in January 1988 and was used in Orpington as fleet number MRL069. It passed to Stagecoach East London in 1994 and was later transferred to the A1 fleet the following year. This view sees it operating an Irvine local service.

BSG 547W was a Leyland Tiger TRCTL11/3R/Duple Dominant III C46Ft, new as Eastern Scottish XH 547 in July 1981. It passed briefly through Midland Scottish hands to become Kelvin Scottish T130X and later 4301. It was re-registered as WLT 742, then WGB 176W. The bodywork was rebuilt to Dominant IV spec. It passed to Northern Scottish in 1989, and was re-registered as CSU 921, then PSO 178W. Stagecoach Bluebird later transferred it to Stagecoach Western.

D38 UAO was a Mercedes L608D/Reebur B20F, purchased new by Cumberland as their number 38 in January 1987. It was transferred to Scotland to work on the competitive services being introduced in Glasgow, but was sent to work in Ayrshire for Stagecoach A1 instead. It was loading in Irvine town centre on the service to Broomlands.

R103 LSO was a Volvo B10M-62/Plaxton Premiere Interurban C51F, new to Stagecoach Western as their number 103 in October 1997. It was later renumbered to 52425 before disposal to Stuart's of Carluke, where it was re-registered as LSV 380. It is shown in Glasgow while working on service X34.

M100 AAB was a Scania L113CRL/Alexander Strider B51F, new to AA Buses member Dodd's of Troon in August 1994. It passed to Stagecoach with the stage operations and is seen in Irvine. The bus would later serve in Dumfries and Glasgow, becoming number 28955 and re-registered as UIB 3076. Ultimately it would be part of the WEE G, a community-based project that visited deprived areas and was fitted out with computers, etc.

UWV 607S was a Bristol VRT/SL3/6LXB/ECW CO43/31F, new as Southdown number 607 in December 1977. These buses were built as convertible open-tops and could have a roof fitted to work in winter time. It is seen in Rothesay, working on the Isle of Bute tour.

N142 XSA was a Volvo B10M-62/Plaxton Premiere C51F, new as Stagecoach Western number 142 in April 1996. It was later transferred to Glasgow for a spell, but is shown working on an X73 service from Edinburgh to Dumfries. On disposal it moved to McColl's Coaches as their number 4017, and was re-registered as DRZ 1307.

DSD 942V was a Seddon Pennine VII/Alexander T Type C49F, purchased new by Western in September 1979 as fleet number S2942. It is shown later in its life after being refurbished to prolong its service. Only a couple of these coaches received Stagecoach stripes. There was a plan at one time to transfer eight of these to Perth, but it came to nought.

J277 OSJ was a Mercedes 709D/Plaxton Beaver B25F, purchased new by Dodd's of Troon for the AA Buses fleet in April 1992, and would pass to Stagecoach Western Buses with the services in June 1997. It is seen in Ayr resplendent in its new colours. It later saw service in Perth.

M680 SSX was a Volvo B6-50/Alexander Dash B40F purchased new in August 1994. It was one of two at Ayr depot to receive this overall advert for Miller Homes and is shown in Burns Statue Square working the local service to Hayhill. It later worked for Northern Blue of Burnley and South Yorkshire of Ackworth.

N857 VHH was a Volvo Olympian YN2R/Alexander R Type H79F, purchased new in August 1995 and originally part of Stagecoach A1 Service. A batch of twenty were diverted from Cumberland to replace many of the non-standard buses acquired with the A1 Service business. It was part of the main Western fleet by the time of this shot, and based at Ayr depot.

M483 ASW was a Volvo B10M-55/Alexander PS Type DP48F, purchased new by Stagecoach A1 Service in June 1995. It was passing through Irvine on the Coastlink 535 service. The branding had to be removed after a court action by Ashton of Greenock who felt it was too close to their identity. For a short while the buses ran in all-over white before the red stripes and ClydeCoaster branding was applied. The bus was later renumbered to 20511 and would see service with Stagecoach in Glasgow and in the Highlands.

L577 NSB was a Mercedes 709D/Dormobile Routemaker B21FL, purchased new by Arran Transport, Brodick, in October 1993. It passed to Western with the bus side of the business, and was captured on the neighbouring Isle of Bute. Martin-Walter was a long-established firm of harness makers in Folkestone, Kent, that switched to building bespoke bodies for motor cars when horse-drawn vehicles began to disappear. A separate coachbuilding company was incorporated in 1969 and named Dormobile after its best-known post-war product.

T641 KCS was a Volvo B10MA-55/Jonckheere AC72F, delivered new as Stagecoach Western Buses number 193 in May 1999. It is shown leaving Buchanan bus station in Glasgow, heading for Irvine on service X34. This coach would remain in service until after the Commonwealth Games, held in Glasgow in 2014.

OSJ 631R was a Leyland Leopard PSU3C/3R/Alexander Y Type B53F, new as Western SMT L2631 in January 1977. It became a driver trainer in later life, and continued in the role after sale to Whitelaw's of Stonehouse. It was later returned to its former glory in Western SMT colours as a preserved bus, owned by McGill's of Greenock.

D246 NCS was a Dodge S5/Alexander B25F, new as Western Scottish D246 in April 1987, shown here working in Kilmarnock, with Stagecoach A1 Service fleet names applied. On disposal it passed to Fereneze Travel, a Paisley-based company owned by Alan Hill.

Brought in to strengthen the Dodd's fleet when it was acquired, this Leyland National had come from Cumberland and was painted to look like an indigenous vehicle. It is seen on service 14, passing through Irvine town centre on what was the traditional service of AA Buses. The style of fleet name applied had more rounded edges than that used by Dodd's of Troon.

VBA 161S was a Leyland Atlantean AN68A/1R/Northern Counties H75F, new to Greater Manchester PTE as their fleet number 8161 in January 1978. It was one of a batch acquired by Western from GM Buses to cover the collapse of Dickson's of Dumfries. It is seen after transfer to Dunoon depot. On disposal it returned to England to work for City Central of Hull.

L262 VSU was a Mercedes 709D/Dormobile Routemaker B29F, purchased new by Hamilton of Maybole in December 1993. It passed to Stagecoach with the business, and was caught leaving Ayr bus station on service 57, bound for Maybole. Hamilton continued in business as a coach operator for a little while longer.

TMS 404X was a Leyland Leopard PSU3G/4R/Alexander Y Type B53F, new as Alexander (Midland) MPE404 in January 1982. It worked for Kelvin Scottish, Highland Scottish and Fife Scottish before joining Western, and is seen at Cumnock depot. The black window surrounds tended to give these buses a more modern look.

P160 ASA was a Volvo B10M-62/Plaxton Premiere Interurban C51F, new as Western Buses number 160 in August 1996, and allocated to Stranraer depot. It is shown leaving Dumfries on the X75 service, a route that will take it back to its home town. Note the fleet names just show 'Stagecoach', with no reference to Western whatsoever.

GCS 48V was a Leyland Leopard PSU3E/4R/Alexander Y Type B53F, purchased new by Western Scottish as their L48 in April 1980. It survived into the Stagecoach era and looks superb in this view showing off its stripes whilst running in Kilmarnock's one-way system on service 10 to Troon. It would later go to nearby independent Keenan of Coalhall for use on school contracts.

D525 RCK was a Mercedes-Benz L608D/Reebur B20F, new to Ribble in September 1986. It was brought to Scotland for use in Glasgow to operate services in competition with First Glasgow, but when the bus war declined it saw use in Ayrshire. It is seen here on a Kilmarnock Town service to Hurlford.

J604 KCU was a Dennis Dart/Wright Handybus B40F, new to Go Ahead Northern in December 1991. It was one of a batch purchased by Dart Buses and operated under a franchise agreement for Stagecoach Glasgow. The X8/9/10 had been very successful when launched but passenger numbers had been steadily declining, mainly because high-density housing was being demolished and replaced by modern semis. As a cost-cutting measure Dart was subcontracted to operate these services on behalf of Stagecoach and many non-low-floor buses replaced modern Stagecoach vehicles.

TSO 23X was a Leyland Olympian ONLXB/1R/ECW H45/32F, new as Northern Scottish NLO 23 in March 1982. It passed to Stagecoach with the business and was transferred to Perth. Western acquired it later in life, and this view shows it working on a school contract in Troon.

GHV 102N was a Daimler Fleetline CRL6/Park Royal H44/27D, new as London Transport DM1102 in June 1975. In September 1983 it was despatched to Aldenham Works for conversion to open-top and transferred to the sales department as a demonstrator. It received Selkent Travel livery and passed to Stagecoach with the business. It was transferred to Western Scottish as their number 104, and is seen in Ayr.

F648 FGE was a Mercedes 609D/Reebur C23F, delivered new to Worthington of Collingham in May 1988. It passed to Pathfinder of Newark and Argyll Coaches of Wemyss Bay before reaching Clyde Coast Coaches. It carried the registration plate 341AYF briefly, but this was changed to F197 ASD before it passed to Stagecoach. It is shown at Stranraer depot.

B24 CGA was a Volvo Citybus B10M-50/Alexander RV Type H47/37F, purchased new by A1 Service member Robert Meney in March 1985. It served just short of ten years before passing to Stagecoach with the business, and duly received its stripes. It carried A1 fleet names for most of its time but did receive the red Western block names briefly. This view was taken at South Beach, Ardrossan. The bus would later serve with McColl's and DJ International.

OSG 552M was a Leyland Leopard PSU3/3R/Alexander Y Type C49F, new as Scottish Omnibuses ZH552 in January 1974. It became Alexander Midland MPE 232, before transfer to Kelvin Scottish in June 1985. It was quickly sold to Stagecoach of Perth, who offered it, along with five others, to Docherty's of Auchterarder if they would compete with Strathtay Scottish in Perth. The offer was refused and the bus entered service with Magicbus in Glasgow, and was working on the tendered 67 service to Lennox Castle.

X739 JCS was a Dennis Dart SLF/Plaxton Pointer B41F, new to Stagecoach Western in September 2000. It was running on an Ayr local service and would later become 33775 in the national fleet numbering scheme. The Lo-liner brand was used by most subsidiaries on new low-floor buses at this time. Number 405 would later work for Stagecoach in Manchester.

EYE 248V was a Leyland Titan TNLXB2RRSP/Park Royal H68D, new to London Transport (T248) in May 1980. It passed to the privatised Stagecoach East London fleet in September 1994, and was transferred to A1 Service, Kilmarnock, in January 1995. By November 1996 it was in the main Western fleet, and on disposal in August 2001 joined McColl's Coaches of Balloch. In November 2002 it was re-registered as TXI 7843 and sold to Blythswood Motors (dealer) in June 2003.

R503 KSA was a Volvo B10M-55/Alexander PS Type B49F, purchased new in August 1997 by Stagecoach Glasgow. It passed to Western and received this all-over advert for Bus Points. This enabled passengers to collect their used bus tickets and redeem them against a range of goods and services. It was working on service 4, which connected Glasgow to Ayr via Kilmarnock.

This Leyland Leopard PSU3E/4R was fitted with a Plaxton Supreme IV Express C49F body, and was new as London Country number PL29 for use on Green Line express services. It then operated for Stagecoach East Midland as their number 17 in the Midland Travel fleet. Western acquired it in 1995 from Bluebird Buses. You can almost hear the roar as it sweeps past on route X76, and it must be said it looked immaculate.

D525RCK was a Mercedes-Benz L608D/Reebur B20F, new to Ribble in September 1986. It was brought to Scotland for use in Glasgow against First Glasgow, but when the bus war declined it saw use in Ayrshire. It is seen here on a Kilmarnock Town service to Hurlford.

GCS 41V was a Leyland Leopard PSU3E/4R/Alexander Y Type B53F, purchased new by Western Scottish as their L41 in March 1980. It remained in the fleet long enough to pass to Stagecoach and receive its stripes. This view was taken in Dumfries, at Buccleuch Bridge, ready to cross the River Nith on a busy local service to Kenilworth Road.

NCS 121W was a Volvo B10M-61/Duple Dominant IV C46Ft, new to Western Scottish as their number V121 in June 1981 for use on the London service. It was re-bodied by East Lancs in 1994 with a DP51F body after an accident and was photographed in Ayr, heading for Stranraer while working on service 60. Western had originally proposed to re-body nine of these vehicles, but the project was abandoned after Stagecoach gained control of the company. Note that no fleet names are carried.

N852 VHH was a Volvo YN2R/Alexander R Type H47/32F, purchased new by Stagecoach A1 Service as their number 918 in August 1995. It then transferred to the main Western fleet, but was captured working for Stagecoach Glasgow on the X1 service to East Kilbride. Note the Stagecoach Express names carried.

C802 KBT was a Leyland Cub CU435/Optare DP33F, purchased new by West Yorkshire PTE as their fleet number 1802 in May 1986. Western acquired it from Arran Transport and Trading, and it is shown in Dunoon depot, freshly repainted into Stagecoach stripes. In September 1984, Leyland closed its Charles H. Roe bodywork-building business in Leeds. Russell Richardson, a former plant director at Roe, backed by the West Yorkshire Enterprise Board and many redundant former employees, formed Optare in February 1985.

M479 ASW was a Volvo B10M-55/Alexander PS Type DP48F, purchased new by Stagecoach Western in April 1995. It was operating on service 43 bound for New Cumnock when captured. It became 20579 in the later fleet numbering series before transfer to Stagecoach Highlands. On disposal it passed to Keenan of Ayr for further service.

F334 JHS was a Talbot Freeway DP12FL, new to Western in March 1989 as their fleet number T274. It was used on SPT contracts, but is seen in Dumfries later in life, wearing Stagecoach livery. The Talbot Express Pullman was a triaxle; early models were built by the company's subsidiary, Rootes of Maidstone, but to keep up with demand, production was shifted to the old Humber car-assembly plant in Coventry. Production rights were later sold to Turner Brown Precision Engineering (TBP) at Bilston, near Wolverhampton.

This MCW Metrorider was new to Fife Scottish and used on local services around Kirkcaldy. It passed with some of its sisters to Ayrshire and was operated on routes of the former A1 Service Co-operative. This view was taken in Irvine. It later joined PANDH Travel of Birkenhead for further service.

FDV 840V was a Bristol VRT/ECW H43/31F, purchased new by Western National as their fleet number 1196 in June 1980. It passed to Devon General before purchase by Stagecoach, and is seen in Bath Street in Glasgow, working for Magicbus. This business was sold to Kelvin Central Buses, but the company would return to the Glasgow bus scene in due course.

H466 WGG was a Scania N113CRB/Alexander PS Type B51F, purchased new by AA member Dodd's of Troon in August 1990. It passed to Stagecoach with the services in June 1997 and is seen in Irvine town centre in ClydeCoaster livery, before the red bands were applied. It was later used at Prestwick Airport, which was also owned by Stagecoach at the time.

G569 ESD was a Volvo B10M-55/Plaxton Derwent B55F, delivered new to A1 Service member Ian Duff. It was caught skirting the seashore at South Beach on its way to Ardrossan. G569 ESD has donned its stripes for this shot and has been re-registered into the bargain as WLT 439. However it looks magnificent and well cared for as it heads for Ardrossan, Chapelhill Mount. It would later serve with Western, Bluebird, Dunn-Line and Veolia Cymru.

KKY 222W was a Bristol VRT/ECW H74F, new to East Midland as their fleet number 222 in May 1981. It was pressed into service after Stagecoach acquired A1 Service, and had to replace many non-standard types quickly. Orders were placed for new buses but some borrowed buses had to plug the gap until they could be delivered. 222 was photographed passing through Irvine town centre whilst bound for Kilmarnock.

K209 KHS was a Mercedes-Benz 709D/Dormobile Routemaker B29F, delivered new to Clyde Coast in March 1993 and remained in the fleet until September 1995, when it passed with the service work to Stagecoach A1 Service. It was originally given the fleet number 269 but this was later changed to 272. After a period of operation with Stagecoach Western, it was sold to Docherty of Auchterarder in 1999 and moved to Moffat and Williamson the following year.

J919 LEM was a Volvo B10M-60/Plaxton Expressliner C46Ft, delivered new to Amberline of Speke in October 1991. The original Expressliner was a Plaxton Paramount III 3500 built to National Express specification, easily recognisable from the standard Paramount by having a windowless rear end incorporating the National Express logo. It came to Western via Ribble, and was on a private hire to Glasgow Green.

TBC 1X was a Leyland Leopard PSU3F/4R/Plaxton Supreme C53F, new to Leicester Corporation in November 1981. On disposal it moved to Nottingham City Transport, then passed to Busways and found its way to their Blue Bus subsidiary. On acquisition by Stagecoach it was transferred to Western in June 1997 and was re-registered as WLT 749 in October 1999.

P889 MNE was a Volvo B10M-55/Northern Counties B48F, purchased new by Stagecoach Western as their number 527 in April 1997, although it had been diverted from a Hampshire Bus order during the Glasgow bus wars. It would later pass to Stagecoach in Wales and be renumbered as 20889. It was arriving in Glasgow while working on the X1 service from East Kilbride.

D917 GRU was a Bedford YMT/Plaxton Derwent B53F, purchased new by Tillingbourne Bus of Cranleigh in March 1987. It later came to the Arran Transport and Trading Company in 1991, and is shown at Cumnock depot complete with Stagecoach Western fleet names.

P375 DSA was a Volvo B6LE-53/Alexander ALX200 DP36F, purchased new by Stagecoach Glasgow in April 1997. It would later pass to Western for use in Ayrshire, in AA Buses livery. On disposal in October 2010 it would join McColl's Coaches as their number 2048. It is shown at Irvine while working on a local service to Perceton.

GSO 77V was a Leyland Leopard PSU3E/4R/Alexander B53F, purchased new by Northern Scottish as their NPE77 in December 1979. It passed to Highland Scottish as number L212 in 1981 and survived into Highland Country days, being up-seated in the process to B55F. In a strange move it was purchased by Stagecoach Western in 1996 and sent to Arran for use as a school bus. This view shows it having just arrived in Brodick.

N865 VHH was a Volvo Olympian YN2RC16V3/Alexander R Type H47/32F, delivered new to Stagecoach A1 Service as their number 931 in September 1995. It looks superb after a repaint into the blue and cream livery as it loads in Irvine. It would later work for Stagecoach in Fife, including a spell with the Rennie's of Dunfermline fleet.

P199 OSE was a Volvo B10MA-55/Plaxton Interurban AC71F, delivered new in December 1996. It is seen whilst working on the X76 service to Cumnock. It later moved to Stagecoach Bluebird and was re-registered as 127 ASV, later receiving school bus yellow livery. On disposal it passed to Watt's Coaches via the Ensign dealership.

B461 FCS was used briefly as a driver trainer and is shown in Kilmarnock's one-way system. I took my own PSV test in Kilmarnock many years ago in a manual Leopard, and can always recall a particularly tight traffic island that I used to dread passing, but on the morning of my test I found, much to my relief, that the council had removed it! B461 FCS was a Dodge/Wadham Stringer, which I believe originated with the military and not a 'proper bus'.

G262 EHD was a DAF SB2305/Plaxton Paramount C53F, purchased new by Arran Transport and Trading of Brodick in October 1989. It passed to Stagecoach Western with the business, and was re-registered as VLT 54 for a spell. It later moved to Stagecoach Bluebird, before disposal to Pegasus of Perth.

N608 VSS leads a convoy of buses through Ayr town centre. It was a Mercedes-Benz 709D/ Alexander Sprint B25F, delivered new to Western in January 1996. The routes in Ayr have changed quite a few times since these days. Bringing up the rear were a pair of Alexander Dash-bodied Volvo B6s.

GSO 8V was a Leyland National NL106L11/1R B44F, purchased new by Northern Scottish as their NPN8 in April 1980. It passed to Strathtay Scottish in June 1985 as their SN5. It would return to Northern, and was re-registered later as KRS 542V. It passed to Stagecoach with the business and was transferred to Western in 1993, and was snapped in Ayr while working on the Girvan service.

E637 DCK was a Renault S46/Dormobile B25F, purchased new by Ribble as their 637 in September 1987. It saw service with Stagecoach Southdown and Stagecoach Fife before joining Western, and was captured at Dumfries MOT testing station at Catherinefield.

E864 RCS was a Volvo Citybus B10M-50/Alexander RV Type CH66F, purchased new by Western Scottish as their V264 in November 1987. It passed to Stagecoach with the business, and is shown in Ayr, wearing an advert for West FM – the local radio station. The station broadcasts from studios in Clydebank, along with sister station Clyde 1 via transmitters in Darvel, Girvan, and Toward Point. The station is owned and operated by Bauer Radio and forms part of the Hits Radio Network.

GCS 53V was a Leyland Leopard PSU3E/4R/Alexander Y Type B53F, delivered new as Western Scottish L53 in April 1980. It is seen arriving in Kilmarnock shortly after receiving Stagecoach stripes, and it has to be said, looking immaculate.

E93 LHG was a Mercedes Benz 709D/Alexander B25F, purchased new by Burnley & Pendle as their fleet number 93 in April 1988. It passed to Stagecoach Ribble as number 793 with the business and was transferred to Western in 1998. It was working on an Irvine local service. On disposal it passed to M&M of Accrington.

WFS 147W was a Leyland Leopard PSU3F/4R/Alexander Y Type B53F, new as Fife Scottish FPE147 in October 1980. It passed to Stagecoach with the business, and was later transferred to Stagecoach Western. It remained in Ayrshire, moving to Dodd's of Troon in 1999, and was used on school contracts. It would finish its days with Keenan of Coalhall as a source of spares.

WGY 589S was a Leyland National 11351/3R B33T new to British Airways (CO46) in June 1978. It was a very attractive buy for Western as it had a very low mileage. It was purchased in 1993 and rebuilt to B48F. The following year saw it re-registered as UIB 3543. As can be seen, it survived long enough to receive its stripes and was caught scurrying through the traffic in Kilmarnock. On disposal it would regain its original registration number and pass to Coakley of Motherwell.

TSD 157Y was a Dennis Dorchester SDA801/108/Plaxton Paramount Express 3200 C49F, delivered new to Western Scottish in March 1983 as their number N157. It passed to Clydeside Scottish (N457) in June 1985 and back to Western in 1989 (N407) as part of a package to rebalance the finances when Clydeside was sold to its management. It is seen heading for Ayr while working a journey on the 04 service.

GGE 127X was a Volvo B10M-60/Duple Dominant III C46Ft, purchased new by Western Scottish as their number V127 in April 1982, for use on the London service. It was rebuilt to Dominant IV spec with larger side windows to allow its use on shorter routes. It was later re-bodied by East Lancs and has also carried the registrations TOS 550X and ESU 435.

GSO 6V was a Leyland National NL106L11/1R B44F, new as Northern Scottish NPN6 in March 1980. It was later re-registered as KRS 540V, and passed to Stagecoach with the business. It was acquired by Stagecoach Western and looked superb as it passed through Ayr town centre.

B192 CGA was a Volvo B10M-61/Plaxton Paramount 3500 C46Ft, purchased new by Western Scottish as their V192 in April 1985. It was transferred to Fife Scottish in 1987 as their number FV1, and later 592. It was re-registered as 896 HOD and renumbered to 596 to reflect this. It passed to Stagecoach with the business and was transferred to Hampshire Bus. In a strange move it returned to Stagecoach Western in 1995 and was numbered as 186 in the fleet.

VBA 161S was a Leyland Atlantean AN68A/1R/Northern Counties H75F, new to Greater Manchester PTE as their number 8161 in January 1978. It was one of a batch acquired by Western from GM Buses to cover the collapse of Dickson's of Dumfries. It is seen after transfer to Dunoon depot and is engaged on a school contract. On disposal it returned to England to work for City Central of Hull.

P398 BRS was a Dennis Dart SLF/Alexander Dash DP40F, purchased new in December 1996 and is shown working on a Dumfries local. This was the last Dart/Dash to remain in service with Western, being withdrawn in late 2008. In 1996 the low-floor Dennis Dart SLF was launched. In 2001, production passed to TransBus International, during which time it was sold as the TransBus Dart SLF; Alexander Dennis took over production in 2004, renaming the product as the Alexander Dennis Dart SLF.

JTF 971W was a Leyland National NL116AL11/1R B52F, purchased new by the Atomic Energy Research Establishment at Harwell, near Didcot in Oxfordshire, in April 1981. On disposal, in 1989, it passed to Farmer t/a Kent Coach Tours, Ashford. It was acquired by Tillingbourne of Cranleigh in 1992, then Mitchell's of Plean before reaching Western Scottish. It is seen in Kilmarnock.

MCS 138W was a Bedford YMT/Duple Dominant II C53F, purchased new by Arran Coaches, Brodick, in April 1981. It passed to Stagecoach with the business, and was surprisingly repainted. It was re-registered as 703 DYE and used at Rothesay depot for a short time, often being employed on the Mount Stuart shuttles.

H149 CVU was a Volvo B10M-60/Plaxton Paramount Expressliner C46Ft, purchased new by Skyliner of Mossley in August 1990. It became number 1167 in the Ribble fleet before transfer to Stagecoach Western in 1995. It was re-registered as WLT 727 in October 1996, and was caught in Glasgow.

GHV 948N was a Daimler Fleetline CRL6/Park Royal H44/27D, new as London Transport DM948 in October 1974. It was sent to the sales department at Aldenham for conversion for export in October 1982, but was instead converted to open-top. It was used by the charter fleet, and later became part of SELKENT. It passed to Stagecoach Western in August 1995, but was sold to Ensign (dealer) just over a year later and was exported to Seville in Spain in 1999.

TSJ 31S was a Leyland Leopard PSU3D/4R/Alexander Y Type B53F, delivered new as Western SMT L2731 in February 1978. It had become Stagecoach Western number 691 by the time of this photograph. Note some of the beading had been removed to give space for the fleet name. This was applied on the roof cove panels on many buses.

J303 BRM was a Dennis Dart 9.8SDL/Alexander Dash B40F, delivered new as Western Scottish N303 in July 1992. It is believed to have been a diverted order from Cumberland, so even at this time the management of Western Scottish must have been in dialogue with Stagecoach management. It would later pass to West Coast Motors with the Dunoon operations.

BSJ 917T was a Leyland Leopard PSU3E/4R/Alexander Y Type B53F, new as Western SMT number L2917 in July 1979. It had a very long career with Western, lasting into Stagecoach days. Unusually it received an all-over advert for Mogil Motors, a local Ford dealer based around Dumfries.

UHG 728R was a Leyland National 11351A/1R B49F, new as Ribble number 728 in September 1976. It later became Sheafline of Sheffield number 885, before purchase by Volvo Bus and Coach. It was repowered with a Volvo engine and used as a demonstrator. It was undergoing inspection at Nursery Avenue in Kilmarnock.

E867 RCS was a Volvo Citybus B10M-50/Alexander RV Type CH45/35F, new as Western Scottish V267 in December 1987. There were originally to be six buses in this batch, but two were diverted to Fife Scottish. Ultimately all would come into Stagecoach ownership. V267 is seen loading in Union Street in Glasgow, while working on service 04, bound for Ayr.

D167 TRA was a Bedford YMT/Duple Dominant B55F, purchased new by British Coal, South Normanton, for staff transport in August 1986. It passed to Arran Coaches in 1991 for competitive services registered against Western Scottish on both Bute and Dunoon, and was taken into stock by Stagecoach with the business.

GCS 60V was a Leyland Leopard PSU3E/4R/Alexander Y Type B53F, purchased new by Western Scottish as their fleet number DL60 in May 1980. It had just received its stripes when captured at Ayr many years later, and looked pristine. The red block-style of fleet name looked good with the stripes.

D122 NUS was a Mercedes L608D/Alexander B21F, purchased new by Kelvin Scottish as their number 1122 in August 1986, and sold to Western Scottish in 1987. It was one of a pair of Mercedes minibuses given this style of advert for the Kyle Shopping Centre in Ayr and was working on local service A2 to Hayhill.

P154 ASA was a Volvo B10M-62/Plaxton Premiere Interurban C51F, purchased new by Western as their number 154 in August 1996. It was passing through Stevenson on the X16 service to Edinburgh. It would later be renumbered as 52354, and was eventually sold to Alpine Coaches of Llandudno.

M789 PRS was originally intended to be Stagecoach Glasgow number 089. It was a Volvo B10M-55/Alexander PS Type DP48F, delivered new to the company in November 1994 and is seen in Union Street in Glasgow, while working on service 4 to Ayr, looking superb with its distinctive red block fleet names.

L578 NSB was a Mercedes 709D/Dormobile Routemaker B21FL, delivered new to Arran Transport, Brodick, in November 1993. It passed to Stagecoach with the business, and is shown operating on Bute. The bodywork seemed to need a lot of attention and strengthening as time went on.

Q138 RDS was an AEC Matador heavily rebuilt by Western SMT. It survived long enough to pass to Stagecoach. It was based on the Scottish island of Arran and is seen here at Brodick. To my mind the stripes sit rather uncomfortably on this classic design, which should have received a more sympathetic livery.

YFS 304W was a Leyland National NL116L11/1R B52F that had begun life with Eastern Scottish as their number N304 in January 1981, before purchase by Central Scottish as number N64 in 1985, and Kelvin Scottish number 1274 in 1986. It finally reached Western in 1988, and later received AA Buses livery in Stagecoach days.

D317 SGB was a Leyland Tiger TRCTL11/3RZ/Duple 340 C49Ft, new to Central Scottish as fleet number C17 in May 1987. It passed to Kelvin Central Buses as number 4307 in 1989. Western purchased it in 1990 and re-registered it as 13 CLT. It was seen in Kilmarnock heading for Ayr on service 4.

C800 HCS was a Leyland Olympian ONLXB/1R/ECW H77F, new to A1 Service member Hill of Stevenston in March 1986, and lasted until January 1995, before passing to Stagecoach with the services. After serving in Ayrshire it was transferred to Stagecoach Glasgow for use on services in the city, later returning to Western once again. It was caught turning out of Ayr bus station.

P150 ASA was a Volvo B10M-62/Plaxton Premiere Interurban C51F, purchased new by Stagecoach Western as their number 150 in August 1996. It was captured in Ayr as it headed for Muirkirk on service 46. It would later be renumbered to fleet number 52350, and on disposal passed to McColl's Coaches.

M949 EGE was a Dennis Dart 9.8SDL/Plaxton Pointer B40F, purchased new by Dodd's of Troon for their AA Buses fleet in December 1994. It passed to Stagecoach with the business in June 1997, and was allocated fleet number 400. It was initially repainted into AA Buses green and cream, but was later treated to corporate stripes as shown in this view taken in Ayr.

Western Scottish B202 CGA was a Dennis Dorchester SDA810/Plaxton Paramount 3500 C55F body, new in July 1985 as number N202. It was re-registered as VLT 272 as shown in the shot, taken in Buchanan bus station in Glasgow. It was carrying Stagecoach express decals as it worked a journey on service X77.

J310 BRM was a Dennis Dart/Alexander Dash B40F, new as Western Scottish Buses number N310 in July 1992, shown at Brodick on the Isle of Arran. Note the parcels at the front of the bus. It would later be acquired by West Coast Motors and see service on the Isle of Bute.

M100 AAB was a Scania L113CRL/Alexander Strider B51F, new to AA Buses member Dodd's of Troon in August 1994. It passed to Stagecoach with the stage operations and is seen in Greenock, having just arrived on service 585 ClydeCoaster from Ayr. The bus would later serve in Dumfries and Glasgow, becoming number 28955 with re-registration number UIB 3076.

KYV 410X was a Leyland Titan TNLXB2RR H66D, new to London Transport as number T410 in January 1982. It passed to Stagecoach SELKENT with the business, and was transferred to Western in 1995. This view sees it leaving Glasgow's Buchanan bus station on a short-working of service 4, which had been beefed up to compete with First Glasgow during the Glasgow bus wars.

M151 FGB was a Volvo B10B-58/Wright Endurance B51F, new to A1 Service member Docherty of Irvine in November 1994 as M1ABO. This was a cherished number plate which stood for 'Ayrshire bus owners'. The original plate was retained by the Docherty family when the services were taken over by Stagecoach in 1995. The bus is seen just out of the paint shop in this view taken at Ardrossan depot on its delivery run. Thankfully it has returned to the Docherty family for preservation.

A317 ONE was a Leyland Tiger TRCTL11/3R/Plaxton Paramount C57F, new to Chesterfield Corporation as their number 4 in 1984. It passed to Stagecoach-owned East Midland with the business and was transferred to Western in 1995. Kilmarnock was the location, and this coach fitted in well with the style employed by Western on their Dorchester Coaches.

M590 PRS was a Volvo B10M-55/Alexander PS Type DP48F, originally intended to·be Stagecoach Glasgow fleet number 090, but delivered instead to Western in November 1994 as their number V590. It was caught passing through Irvine on its way to Kilmarnock whilst working on service 21.

J14 WSB was purchased new by Western Scottish in May 1992 and was a Dennis Javelin/Plaxton Paramount 3200 C53F. It was seen in Stranraer depot while getting washed and fuelled by the shunters. On disposal it would pass to Semmence Coaches based in Norfolk.

An interesting line-up of ex-A1 Service Leyland Olympians with their new masters. We tend to think of the standard livery being applied, but just look at the variations. These buses were very reliable and would last for quite a long time.

OSJ 636R was a Leyland Leopard PSU3C/3R/Alexander Y Type B53F, new as Western SMT L2636 in February 1977. It was sold to Chesterfield Transport, and returned to Western under Stagecoach control. It was converted to open-top for use on Arran, but was later sold to Lothian Buses, then passed to City Sightseeing for tours of Belfast.

OHV 762Y was an all-Leyland Titan TNLXB2RR H44/24D, new as London Transport T762 in April 1983. In September 1994 it passed to Stagecoach Selkent, and March 1996 would see it move to Stagecoach Glasgow as their fleet number 955. It was sent to join the main Western fleet in February 1998, and is shown working in Dumfries.

E159 XHS was a Volvo B10M-56/Duple 300 series B53F, purchased new by Hutchison's of Overtown in February 1988. It left the fleet in March 1994 to join A1 Service member Docherty's of Irvine, and entered service the following month. Its tenure would be short-lived however as Stagecoach took over in January 1995. It was numbered as V598 and was re-registered in April as WLT 538. It would eventually become 20598 in the national fleet numbering sequence.

N617 USS was a Volvo B10M-62/Plaxton Expressliner C44Ft, new as Stagecoach Western number 617 in September 1995, shown here resting between duties at Stranraer depot in National Express livery. It would receive fleet number 52306 in the national fleet numbering series. It would pass to Stagecoach Bluebird, Hookways of Meeth, Mid-Devon Coaches and Edwards of Llantwit Fardre.

B577 LPE was a Leyland Olympian ONTL11/2RSp/ECW CH45/28F, new in January 1985 to Alder Valley. It passed to Clyde Coast in July 1991 and lasted just over a year. On withdrawal in August 1982 it passed to Cleveland Coaches and was re-registered as PJI 4983. In July 1995 it moved to Stagecoach Western. It was sold to Stephenson's of Rochford in 1999 and then to Tim's Travel of Sheerness in 2000.

G575 YTR was a Fiat 49.10/Pheonix B25F, purchased new by A1 Service of Ardrossan in July 1990. The idea was that to spread the risk of minibus operation, they would be owned by the company itself and not individual members. G575 YTR passed to Stagecoach with the business and was allocated to Stranraer for a spell.

M726 BCS was a Volvo B6-50/Alexander Dash DP40F, purchased new by Stagecoach Western in August 1994. It was photographed in Ardrossan whilst working on service 11 on a sunny Sunday afternoon. It carried the fleet number KV326, but this was later simplified to just 326.

XSJ 668T was a Leyland Fleetline FE30AGR/Northern Counties H44/31F, purchased new by Western Scottish as their R2787 in April 1979. It passed to Clydeside Scottish in June 1985, but later returned to Western and was one of the few to receive Stagecoach stripes. It is seen in Stranraer depot. Many of these buses were replaced by Leyland Titans cascaded from London.

G344 FFX was a Volvo B10M-60/Plaxton Paramount C46Ft, purchased new by Dorset Travel services in June 1990. It was acquired by Stagecoach Western in 1995 and is shown freshly repainted at Cumnock. It later received a white livery to replace coaches owned by Owen's of Chapelhall after Stagecoach purchased the Scottish Highway Express business. It later carried the registration plate transferred from WLT 909.

Western Scottish received a batch of ten Alexander Dash-bodied Dennis Darts, diverted from a Stagecoach Cumberland order. This was perhaps a clue that Stagecoach would go on to purchase the company from its management. Four of the batch are lined up here at Ardrossan depot. One was withdrawn after an accident, but the remaining nine would ultimately pass to West Coast Motors.

D526 ESG was a Leyland Tiger TRCTL11/3RH/Duple 340 C46Ft, new as Fife Scottish FLT26 in April 1987. It was re-registered as MSU 466 and passed to Stagecoach with the business, later becoming Stagecoach South number 1066. It was added to the Western fleet in 1996, and is shown in Wellington Street in Glasgow working on the X76 service bound for Kilmarnock.

GYE 281W was a Leyland Titan TNLXB2RR H44/24D, purchased new by London Regional Transport as their T281 in July 1981. It passed to the privatised East London Company in September 1994, before disposal to Stagecoach A1 Service in January 1995. It had become Stagecoach Western by October 1995 and is seen here in Kilmarnock. It moved back down south in September 2000 to work in Lancaster. Three years later it was converted to open top to work on The Lakeland Experience.

B47 DWE was a Leyland Tiger TRCTL11/3RH/Plaxton Paramount II C51F, new to East Midland as their number 47 in April 1985. It passed to Stagecoach Bluebird as number 469 in 1994 and was later transferred to Western. It was captured leaving Glasgow's Buchanan bus station bound for Stranraer.

NCS 121W was a Volvo B10M-61/Duple Dominant IV C46Ft, new to Western Scottish in June 1981, but was re-bodied by East Lancs in 1994 with a DP51F body after an accident and was photographed in Irvine whilst working the ClydeCoaster. Note that the spelling of Wemyss Bay is wrong on the route branding on the front of the bus.

B421 CMC was a Leyland Tiger TRCTL11/3RH/Plaxton Paramount 3200 C53F, new in 1985 to Chesterfield Corporation as their number 1 and passed with the business to Stagecoach East Midland. It was one of five vehicles transferred to Western in 1995, and was caught leaving Glasgow's Buchanan bus station en route to Thornhill on a peak hour express working.

This was Western preparing for the Glasgow bus war with a good selection of the available vehicles ready for action at Kilmarnock depot. The depot was built by Scottish Transport, and had workshops attached, remaining in use after Western SMT was formed. Part of the site was sold off in Stagecoach days for housing, and the head office relocated to Sandgate, Ayr.

PJI 4983 (B577LPE) was transferred to Ayr depot to work on the Butlin's WonderWest contract and received this attractive livery. It is seen leaving Ayr bus station on the Butlin's service on a lovely summer's day. Butlin's was founded by Billy Butlin to provide affordable holidays for ordinary British families, and between 1936 and 1966, ten camps were built. In 1998 the camp at Ayr was rebranded as Haven Park, and operated as Craig Tara by Haven since 1999.

B402OSB (GSU 950) was a Dennis Dorchester SDA810/Plaxton Paramount 3500 C55F, new to Clydeside Scottish (402) in July 1985. When Clydeside was privatised it was one of a number of assets sold to Western to pay off the purchase price. B197CGA (WLT 697) was a Volvo B10M-61/Plaxton Paramount C46Ft, purchased new by Western Scottish as their V197 in May 1985. Both were captured together at Stranraer Depot.

RRM 383X was a Leyland National NL116AL11/1R B52F, purchased new by Cumberland as their number 383 in November 1981. It passed briefly to Stagecoach Western to strengthen the fleet after AA Buses sold out. It is shown working on the former AA Service as it arrives in Ayr. I believe it returned to Cumberland before eventual disposal to Serverse Travel of Tamworth.

Also included at that time was Clydeside's share of the Glasgow to Kilmarnock service and these high-floor coaches. Seen again here, GSU 950 lasted long enough to pass to Stagecoach and is seen gaining its stripes at Kilmarnock Works. The Stagecoach livery was very clever in that all the colours could be applied at the same time and once dried the white lines were applied, and this really lifted it.

RFS 579V was a Leyland National LN11611/1R B52F, new as Eastern Scottish N579 in April 1980. It was transferred to Central Scottish in June 1985 becoming N55 in that fleet. It was not destined to remain long, however, as it moved on to Kelvin Scottish as number 1219 the following year. It moved to Western Scottish as part of a batch of twenty in 1988 and lasted into Stagecoach days. This view sees it operating on the Isle of Arran leaving Brodick after meeting the ferry from Ardrossan.

TSJ 71S was new to Western SMT in December 1977 as their fleet number L2711 and was a Leyland Leopard PSU3D/4R/Alexander Y Type B53F. It survived long enough to get Stagecoach stripes, and was caught in Ayr bus station while working on the service to Girvan.

One of the earliest repaints into Stagecoach was WLT 727, shown in Jamaica Street in Glasgow while operating a journey on service 4. No fleet names were carried initially, but fleet numbers were applied in the usual Western fashion. The first letter was the depot code, followed by the type of bus. This coach was originally registered as TSD 155Y, and was a Plaxton Paramount-bodied Dennis Dorchester SDA801/106.

M721 BCS was a Volvo B6-50/Alexander Dash DP40F, new to Western in August 1994. On disposal it became Ferrymill Motors number FM12 and ran on loan to various companies. When Ferrymill sold it, it went to City Sprinter and ran in Glasgow for a while. However it was caught in Kilmarnock in this view, working on a local service.